D1271364

MY HOME, YOUR HOME, OUR HOMES

By EMMA CARLSON BERNE

Illustrations by ERIN TAYLOR

Music by ERIK KOSKINEN

CANTATA
LEARNING

WWW.CANTATALEARNING.COM

CANTATA
LEARNING

Published by Cantata Learning
1710 Roe Crest Drive
North Mankato, MN 56003
www.cantatalearning.com

Library of Congress Cataloging-in-Publication Data
Names: Berne, Emma Carlson, author. | Taylor, Erin, 1984- illustrator. |
 Koskinen, Erik, composer.
Title: My home, your home, our homes / by Emma Carlson Berne ; illustrations
 by Erin Taylor ; music by Erik Koskinen.
Description: North Mankato, MN : Cantata Learning, 2019. | Series: How are we
 alike and different? | Audience: K to Grade 3.
Identifiers: LCCN 2017056427 (print) | LCCN 2018001946 (ebook) | ISBN
 9781684102655 (eBook) | ISBN 9781684102396 (hardcover : alk. paper) | ISBN
 9781684102914 (paperback : alk. paper)
Subjects: LCSH: Dwellings--Juvenile literature.
Classification: LCC GT172 (ebook) | LCC GT172 .B49 2019 (print) | DDC
 392.3/6--dc23
LC record available at https://lccn.loc.gov/2017056427

Book design and art direction, Tim Palin Creative
Editorial direction, Kellie M. Hultgren
Music direction, Elizabeth Draper
Music arranged and produced by Erik Koskinen

Printed in the United States of America.
0390

ACCESS THE MUSIC!

SCAN
CODE
WITH
MOBILE
APP

CANTATALEARNING.COM

TIPS TO SUPPORT LITERACY AT HOME

WHY READING AND SINGING WITH YOUR CHILD IS SO IMPORTANT

Daily reading with your child leads to increased academic achievement. Music and songs, specifically rhyming songs, are a fun and easy way to build early literacy and language development. Music skills correlate significantly with both phonological awareness and reading development. Singing helps build vocabulary and speech development. And reading and appreciating music together is a wonderful way to strengthen your relationship.

READ AND SING EVERY DAY!

TIPS FOR USING CANTATA LEARNING BOOKS AND SONGS DURING YOUR DAILY STORY TIME

1. As you sing and read, point out the different words on the page that rhyme. Suggest other words that rhyme.

2. Memorize simple rhymes such as Itsy Bitsy Spider and sing them together. This encourages comprehension skills and early literacy skills.

3. Use the questions in the back of each book to guide your singing and storytelling.

4. Read the included sheet music with your child while you listen to the song. How do the music notes correlate to the words of the song?

5. Sing along on the go and at home. Access music by scanning the QR code on each Cantata book. You can also stream or download the music for free to your computer, smartphone, or mobile device.

Devoting time to daily reading shows that you are available for your child. Together, you are building language, literacy, and listening skills.

Have fun reading and singing!

Homes can be many different places. A wood house in a town can be a home. An apartment in a tall building in the city can be a home. A grass or mud hut way out in the country can be a home as well! Some homes can move, like a **yurt** or a trailer. No matter how different homes are, they all give us **shelter** from the hot sun, the wind, or cold snow. Let's sing together about our homes!

4

Is your house made of brick,
with others all around?

Does it have a porch and stairs
and floors both up and down?

Big or small, short or tall,
our homes, they are the same.

They keep us safe from a storm,
or snow or sun or rain.

An apartment is a home
in a building oh so tall.

It's **cozy** high above the street,
with **neighbors** down the hall.

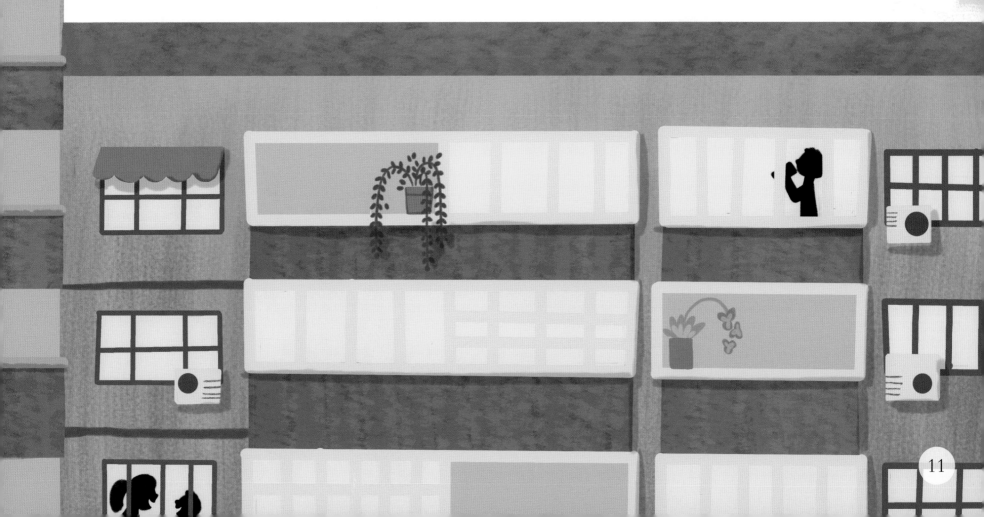

Big or small, short or tall,
our homes, they are the same.

They keep us safe from a storm,
or snow or sun or rain.

12

Is your home made of grass,
a hut so round and small?

There's room enough for everyone
within its woven walls.

Big or small, short or tall,
our homes, they are the same.

They keep us safe from a storm,
or snow or sun or rain.

Adobe homes stand strong
upon the desert sands.

Their thick mud walls will keep you cool
in hot southwestern lands.

Big or small, short or tall,
our homes, they are the same.

They keep us safe from a storm,
or snow or sun or rain.

SONG LYRICS
My Home, Your Home, Our Homes

Is your house made of brick,
with others all around?
Does it have a porch and stairs
and floors both up and down?

Big or small, short or tall,
our homes, they are the same.
They keep us safe from a storm,
or snow or sun or rain.

An apartment is a home
in a building oh so tall.
It's cozy high above the street,
with neighbors down the hall.

Big or small, short or tall,
our homes, they are the same.
They keep us safe from a storm,
or snow or sun or rain.

Is your home made of grass,
a hut so round and small?
There's room enough for everyone
within its woven walls.

Big or small, short or tall,
our homes, they are the same.
They keep us safe from a storm,
or snow or sun or rain.

Adobe homes stand strong
upon the desert sands.
Their thick mud walls will keep you cool
in hot southwestern lands.

Big or small, short or tall,
our homes, they are the same.
They keep us safe from a storm,
or snow or sun or rain.

My Home, Your Home, Our Homes

Americana with World Influence
Erik Koskinen

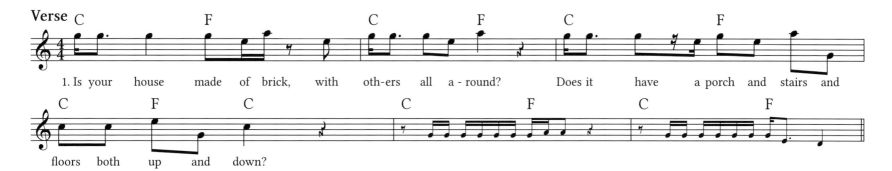

Verse

1. Is your house made of brick, with oth-ers all a - round? Does it have a porch and stairs and floors both up and down?

Chorus

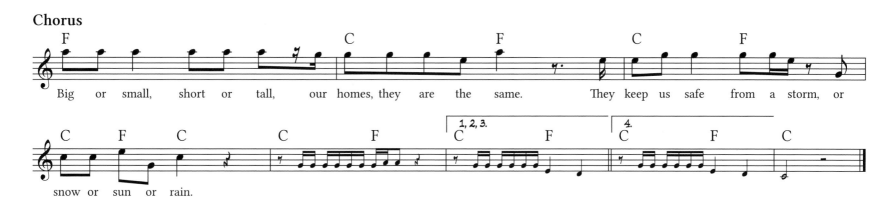

Big or small, short or tall, our homes, they are the same. They keep us safe from a storm, or snow or sun or rain.

Vere 2
An apartment is a home
in a building oh so tall.
It's cozy high above the street,
with neighbors down the hall.

Chorus

Vere 3
Is your home made of grass,
a hut so round and small?
There's room enough for everyone
within its woven walls.

Chorus

Vere 4
Adobe homes stand strong
upon the desert sands.
Their thick mud walls will keep you cool
in hot southwestern lands.

Chorus

GLOSSARY

adobe—a kind of brick made from dried mud or clay

cozy—warm and relaxing

neighbors—people who live near you

shelter—protection

yurt—a kind of round tent used by people in parts of Mongolia and Siberia

CRITICAL THINKING QUESTIONS

1. This song describes homes from different parts of the world. How would you describe your own home? Draw a picture!

2. Look back through the book. Name one way that homes are the same all over the world.

3. Have you ever wanted to live in kind of home that is different than yours? What kind of home would you like to try sleeping in one day? What seems fun or interesting about that kind of home?

TO LEARN MORE

Lamothe, Matt. *This Is How We Do It: One Day in the Lives of Seven Kids from around the World.* San Francisco: Chronicle Books, 2017.

McDowell, Pamela. *Where Do You Live? Farm.* New York: Av2 by Weigl, 2015.

Saunders, Catherine, Katy Lennon, and Sam Priddy. *Children Just Like Me: A New Celebration of Children around the World.* London: DK Children, 2016.